Parents, teachers, mentors, life coach
of teaching children to practice good life
sition from childhood to productive adu
pursuing life goals, maintaining a healthy lifestyle, and getting along with others, are just a few critical tasks that must be performed well everyday. Likewise, many adults of all ages take on the challenge of personal-development, by taking charge of their lives and striving to improve skillset.

In his book, *Life is What You Make It*, Mr. Hardge appeals to the power within each individual to control their own destiny, by enhancing their thoughts and behaviors. Through a combination of self reflections, inspirational words from notable world changers, music and video, Mr. Hardge offers a plethora of practical skills for proud, productive and powerful living, that are easy to understand and remember. His 22 creation principles are impactful and beneficial to individuals of all ages. Whether you are an individual looking to help a child develop a firm foundation, an adult looking for a fresh start, or a person looking to continuously improve one's self, as the start of the next phase of their personal growth, this book is for you.

—**Brian C. Johnson**, MBA, Vice Mayor, City of West Park, President/CEO, Minority Builders Coalition, Inc., Member of Omega Psi Phi Fraternity, Inc.

The Principles shared by Mr. Hardge are pithy, but powerful, profound, and practical. He creatively captivates the reader with a perspective that informs and inspires a generation that will be challenged and changed by reading this book and listening to the music of Mr. Hardge.

—**Dr. Marcus D. Davidson**, Senior Pastor,
New Mt. Olive Baptist Church, Ft. Lauderdale, FL.

Mr. Hardge's book of aspirations, confirmations, Proverbs and Parables are a necessary medium for all of us. However, he has found away to communicate to our youth in a manner that they are comfortable with. How he has chosen to expose this population to worthwhile and valuable information is to be commended. Reading is fundamental, and understanding what you read is the process of education. I'm waiting on volume 2.

—**Bobby Henry**, Westside Gazette

Mr. Hardge's 22 Creation Principles is a recipe for success for young men and women who are looking for opportunities but are void of the information, skills, and confidence to actualize their dreams. Each principle focuses young adults on pertinent thought, action and execution that separate those who dream success and those who achieve success. Using personal testimonies, stories, quotes and play on words, Mr. Hardge gets to the heart of what it takes to win and win BIG.

—**Carletha Shaw**, Educational Professional, Broward County Public Schools,
Member of Delta Sigma Theta Sorority, Inc.

This manuscript, penned by Mr. Hardge, speaks to the power of transformation. This transformation is eloquently illustrated with the maturation of the caterpillar to a butterfly. Mr. Hardge's own life has been transformed through an inward focus and desire to better himself. As a result, he devotes his time and talents to the betterment of others. I applaud Mr. Hardge for his transformation and this book is just one of the many ways Mr. Hardge leverages his God given talents to be a blessing to the world.

—**Dennis Wright**, Chapter President, 2016,
100 Black Men of Greater Ft. Lauderdale

A phenomenal motivational journey delivering sound Step-by-Step nuggets on how to take ownership of how an individual's life turns out. Mr. Hardge has a unique ability to make the reader jump into the illustrative imaginary (Juan and Pookie) and real life narratives…he then backs it up with exercises to immediately capture what has been shared to get it to "stick to the bone" of the reader's thoughts. Finally, he challenges the reader to introspectively face the man in the mirror, and either like what is seen, or have the courage to change it to the image they aspire to be.

—**Sandy James**, Cox Media Consultant

I read *Life is What You Make It* twice in two weeks. This is a book that should be read by every young male and female, who may be dealing with issues associated with peer pressure and living wholesome lives. Mr. Hardge gives the reader true accounts of his own life, and the methods used to change his adversities into positive living skills. Young people will understand the importance of Education, Setting and Achieving Goals, Overcoming Adversity and NEVER giving up. Our youth have major adversities to overcome in our society. However, by following the blueprint set forth by Mr. Hardge, it will give them the resources necessary to overcome obstacles seen and unseen, by teaching them that "Life Is What You Make It" by applying his I AM Principle. Information + Application = Manifestation, which is simply What we Know + What we DO = What we Get.
Great piece of work Mr. Hardge.

—**Beverly Elliott-Morrison**, Retired Lieutenant
Palm Beach Sheriff's Office

Life is What You Make It is an easy, quick read, but profound. The author was startlingly transparent and quite ingenious in his ability to use the parlance of a generation that needs to be heard, understood, and inspired. If you want to change the way you think about yourself, about others and about your condition, *Life is What You Make It*, is a must read!

—**Erhabor Ighodaro**, PhD, Vice Mayor,
City of Miami Gardens

Life is What You Make It depicts a real life account of the obstacles Student-Athletes face through their Academic and Athletic Careers. In most cases, these individuals often lack the proper methods and strategies to overcome the obstacles they are facing. Reading this book will challenge them to evaluate their thoughts, actions, interactions, and surroundings, for which they may become a product of in a positive or sometimes negative manner. Overall, reading this book makes the Student-Athlete evaluate and define where they are in life, and from that, they can determine what they desire to become, and where they would like to fit into society. Great Read!

—**Wesley Frater**, Tournament of Champions, Inc.

A Powerful read right here. Inside the Edu-Tainment Philosophy of Mr. Hardge, this book gives you the Blueprint to turn your negative thinking into a positive one. It allows you to reach deep down into the inner workings of your mind, as well as your thought processes, to channel those negative, fearful, pessimistic thoughts, into a positive outlook within yourself. Life is Definitely What You Make It, and Mr. Hardge has written The 22 Principles To Awaken The Creator Within You, and it is all that and more. If you desire inward and outward Success for yourself, as well as those surrounding you, this Book, CD, and DVD combination will assist you in accomplishing your objectives. It is truly Edu-Tainment at it's best.

—**Terrance "Babyhead" Gibson**, Rho Sigma Chapter President,
Phi Beta Sigma Fraternity, Inc.

Life is What You Make It is a simple, straightforward, to the point, no nonsense approach for anyone who wants to improve their lives and create success for themselves and their community.

—**Dale V.C. Holness**, Broward County District 9 Commissioner

Mr. Hardge has taken the complex subject of life and developed the 22 principles as a roadmap. His eloquent use of language is easy to digest and relate to on any level. I have known Mr. Hardge for more than 15 years and I have watched the transformation and development of his life. The advice intertwined with life experiences is engaging, concise, and provides excellent and relevant examples. This book will appeal not only to those who seek success and personal growth, but to students and business professionals. I congratulate Mr. Hardge on this exceptionally thoughtful, useful and practical principles—I was inspired and motivated.

—**Ms. Garrie Harris**, President, Co-founder Alpha1 Staffing, Search Firm,
www.alpha1staffing.com

**Library of Congress Cataloging-in-Publication Data
is available through the Library of Congress**

© 2017 Mr. Hardge

ISBN-13: 978-0-692--85878-3 (Paperback)
ISBN-10: 0-692-85878-4 (Paperback)

Distinct Publishers, its logos, and marks are trademarks of Distinct Publishers.

Publisher: Distinct Publishers

Cover design by Larissa Hise Henoch
Illustrations by Larissa Hise Henoch
Interior formatting by Larissa Hise Henoch and Lawna Patterson Oldfield

Table of Contents

vii FOREWORD

ix B-FLY STORY

xii ACKNOWLEDGMENTS

xv INWARD CONVERSATIONS, CREATE OUTWARD REALITIES!

1 **CREATION PRINCIPLE 1**
Get Yo Mind Right!

3 **CREATION PRINCIPLE 2**
The 6 Types of People

9 **CREATION PRINCIPLE 3**
Mind Over Matter

15 **CREATION PRINCIPLE 4**
Level of Expectations!

17 **CREATION PRINCIPLE 5**
Law of Adaption!

23 **CREATION PRINCIPLE 6**
Leadership!

27 **CREATION PRINCIPLE 7**
Karma is Looking for You!

31 **CREATION PRINCIPLE 8**
Motivation thru Stimulation!

35 **CREATION PRINCIPLE 9**
Habitual Establishments!

41 **CREATION PRINCIPLE 10**
What You See, is What You Will Be!

43   **CREATION PRINCIPLE 11**
      D-Termination!

45   **CREATION PRINCIPLE 12**
      Success Ain't No Secret!

49   **CREATION PRINCIPLE 13**
      You Are Exactly, Where You Thought You Would Be!

51   **CREATION PRINCIPLE 14**
      The Law of Attraction!

69   **CREATION PRINCIPLE 15**
      Are You Conscious?

71   **CREATION PRINCIPLE 16**
      How I Got Away!

73   **CREATION PRINCIPLE 17**
      Where there' is a Will, there is a Way!

75   **CREATION PRINCIPLE 18**
      How Bad Do You Want It?

77   **CREATION PRINCIPLE 19**
      T+A=R Thoughts + Actions = Reality

81   **CREATION PRINCIPLE 20**
      Co-Creators!

83   **CREATION PRINCIPLE 21**
      The Gift!

85   **CREATION PRINCIPLE 22**
      Neva Give Up!

89   Mr. Hardge's 13 Traits of Highly Successful People

91   Success Test

99   Attitude of Gratitude

Foreward

When I was invited to write the foreward to this book, I viewed it as both and honor and a personal favor to a loyal alumnus of the institution I am privileged to lead—Florida Memorial University. However, I was wholly unprepared for the entirely transformative experience of reading the manuscript. In slightly more than one hundred skillfully constructed pages, "Mr. Hardge" has created what can best be described as "a topical concordance for personal and professional success." This intricately woven tapestry of scripture, motivational images, historic references, scientific facts and a healthy dose of good common sense, create for the reader a clear sense that he or she has the power to fully harness their God-given potential, conquer any fears or insecurities, and quite literally bend the very universe to their will through the power of positive thinking and purposeful action.

As an educator, I believe deeply in the power of education to transform lives. However, what I, and many others in my position, often fail to fully appreciate is that academic success is only part of the equation. Mr. Hardge has gone far below the surface level of formal education to unearth the elements of character, habit, motivation and determination that often make the critical difference between success and failure. The brilliance of the work lies in its simplicity and its authenticity as many of the lessons shared are those learned from his highly improbable life journey.

Early in the work, Mr. Hardge identifies six types of people: pilots, passengers, performers, predators, protégés and partners. While the characteristics of each may at first seem apparent, by the end of the Chapter the reader is left to reflect on both his/her own role in the present and the role they aspire to be. In short, the work pushes you to think, to plan, to aspire and ultimately to achieve!

In a highly technologically sophisticated, fast-paced and increasingly competitive world where the social, economic and psychological noise often drown out positive thinking, spiritual reflection and thoughtful planning, this book is a necessity. I challenge you to read this book with an open mind, clear head and willing heart—you will be so glad you did!

Dr. Rosyln Clark Artis, J.D., President, Florida Memorial University

"I'm walking in my **DESTINY**, found my **ASSIGNMENT**, things that I **VALUE** are the things I spend **TIME** with."

—Mr Hardge

B-Fly Story

There were 2 young Caterpillars named Pookie and Juan who lived in Fort Lauderdale, FL. They were from the inner-city, and filled with big ambition. They were determined to become successful, and were on the ground observing a butterfly hovering over them. Pookie said to Juan, "I would give anything to become a butterfly." Juan said, "me to homie." Suddenly, the butterfly came closer and said, "what up y'all, my name is B-Fly, I overheard what you said about wanting to become a butterfly. If you are willing to grow thru some changes, you can become a butterfly. However, if you don't want to grow thru any changes, you, or your life won't change. The great thing about it is, I can show you how all of it is done." Pookie and Juan looked at each other with faces of concern. Pookie said, "B-Fly, what kind of changes will we have to grow thru?" B-Fly said, "on the way to becoming a butterfly, you are going to have to spend some time all by yourself in solitary confinement, a Cocoon, and you will not have access to the outside world, no text messages, no Instagram, no email, or no cell phone calls. You will have to be willing to make a sacrifice. This sacrifice is not a punishment, but a price you have to pay, in order to prepare you to become a butterfly. During this time period, you should get to know your true self, you should begin to seek your Purpose for growing thru these changes, you should begin to question your mere existence, your reason for living. The type of conversations you have with yourself during this time will determine the type of butterfly you will become, once you fight your way out. Oh yea, nobody is going to let you out, you are going to have to fight your way out of the cocoon. If you don't learn to fight for your freedom, you will never be free, or accomplish anything of great significance. Furthermore, if somebody lets you out, you will not be prepared for the fight in the world that you would be facing. Becoming a butterfly is half the battle, staying alive in the midst of so many predators, and overcoming daily adversities is the other half. Learning to fight for your Dreams, your Purpose, your Goals, your Life, is essential. You will also have to increase your Faith to make it thru this dark time. Faith, is loyalty to an unseen reality. You will have to learn to visualize what life will be like once you get out; this utilization of your imagination is called visualization, and is what is going to get you thru this dark time. Being able to see the light, while you are surrounded by darkness is very important. Being able to see the Best is Yet to come, while you are in a situation that can be perceived as bad is necessary. Remember, As a man thinketh, so is He.

Pookie said, "are you some type of Preacher or Philosopher like D.T. Gates?" B-Fly said "do you mean T.D. Jakes?" Pookie said "Yeah, that's him T.D. Jakes, that man is D-Bomb." B-Fly said "You will learn to rely on yourself thru Faith, because self-preservation is imperative. You will also develop a closer relationship with your creator, because he is the only one you will have access to. Understand young homies, you have to

Go Thru Something, To Get To Something."

As Pookie and Juan looked at each other, B-Fly said, "Come, follow me," and led them into a section of the hood they had never seen. They went under this bridge, and observed dozens of cocoons hanging. Juan said, "B-Fly are those the cocoons?" B-fly said, "yes, these young caterpillars that have made a decision and commitment to change. They believe if they are going to become something different, they had to do something different. What up y'all, what are y'all gonna do?"

This story is indicative of our lives as spiritual individuals Being Human. We desire change around us, but try and avoid the changes needed in our character, our relationships, our habits, our thinking, our decisions and our daily lives to manifest the changes in our reality. Once the caterpillar changes into a butterfly, it will never, go back to being a caterpillar. We need this permanent type of change within us, in order for God to use us as well. The question is, "Are you willing, are you ready?"

"Are you willing, are you ready?"

We can do all things, through Christ
who strengthens us!
—Philippians 4:13

I will work for "EVERYTHING" I pray for, and I will do "EVERYTHING" I can do, to make my dreams come true.

I AM 110% RESPONSIBLE FOR MY LIFE!

xi

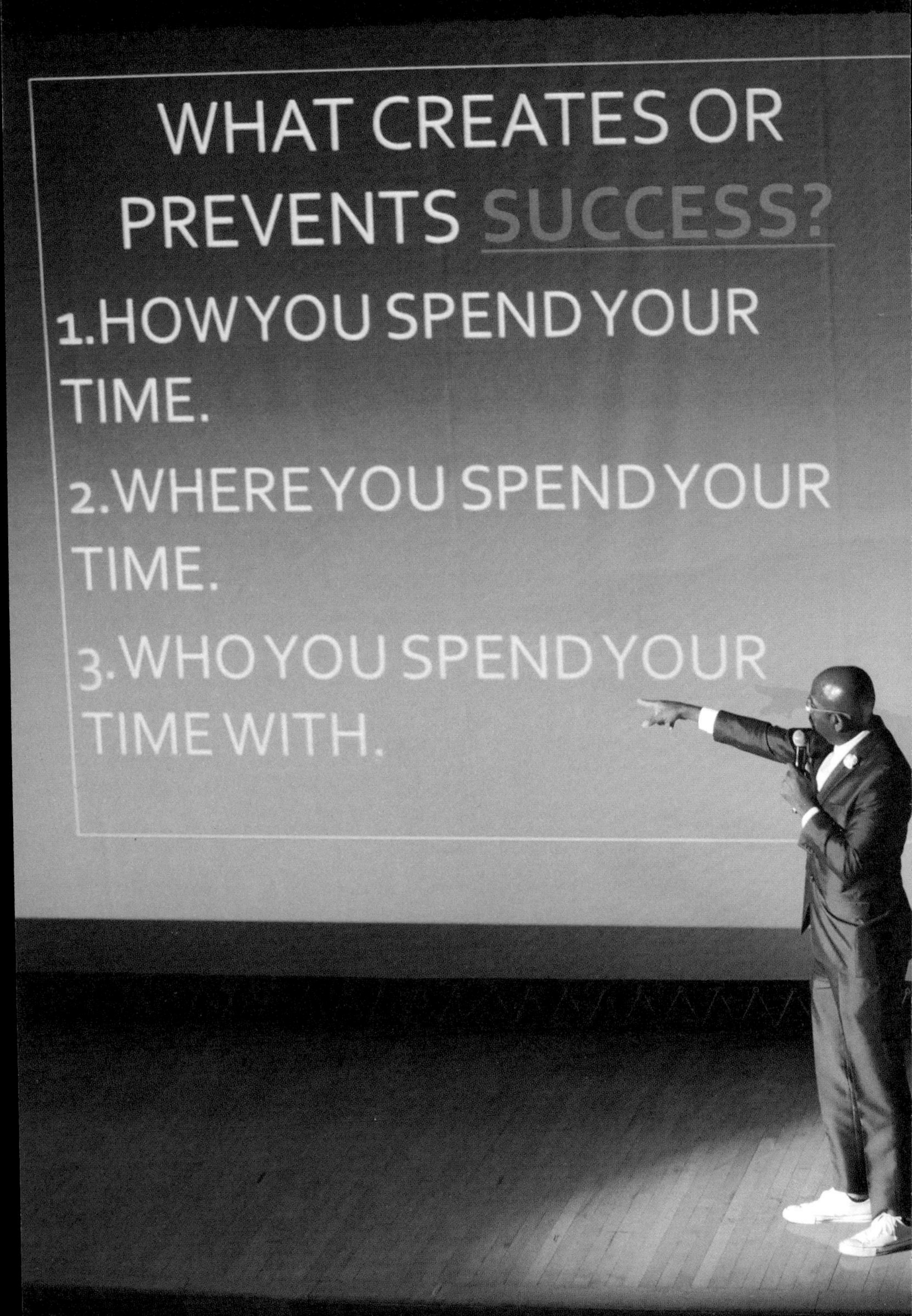
WHAT CREATES OR
PREVENTS SUCCESS?
1.HOW YOU SPEND YOUR
TIME.
2.WHERE YOU SPEND YOUR
TIME.
3.WHO YOU SPEND YOUR
TIME WITH.

Acknowledgments

I would sincerely like to thank God, and my Lord and Savior Jesus Christ, for the many Blessings that have come my way, the greatest being life itself, and allowing me the opportunity to find my Purpose. Also, I am grateful for his favor, and the anointing that has been placed upon my life. My parents, John and Virginia Hardge, who have been, and are still in my corner until this day, I am forever indebted. For I truly believe, the foundation of our civilization, is the family. Princess Darrielle, Super Darrell II, and Dylan The General, I am so proud to be your Father, I live for y'all. To all of my Partners and Supporters that are focused on improving the lives of our youth. Kappa Alpha Psi Fraternity, Inc., Pompano, Fort Lauderdale, Miramar, Miami Alumni Chapters. The 100 Black Men of Greater Fort Lauderdale and Miami, All of the Delta Sigma Theta and Alpha Kappa Alpha Alumni Chapters in Broward, Dade, and Palm Beach Counties. Thanks to my mentors, Rev. Dr. Gregory Bernard Pope and Pastor Amos Benefield, for taking the time to answer all of my questions and concerns. To all of the Teachers, Mentors, Pastors, Clergy, and Coaches. It truly takes a village to raise a child. If the village does not, the streets will.

I have received an unmerited amount of favor since the release of my first manuscript, *Prescription For Success, 17 Principles for Success and Achievement.* Invitations to speak into the lives of our younger generation have not stopped. I will also like to thank Dr. Marcus Davidson of The New Mt. Olive Baptist Church, Bishop Henry Fernandez of the Faith Center, The MTL Program (Mentoring Tomorrows Leaders) of the Broward County Public Schools, specifically Dr. Laurel Thompson and Mrs. Shirley Baker, President of Florida Memorial University, Dr. Roslyn Artis. My Alma Mater, Coach Kenny "Spider" Bellinger, Mrs. Peggy Martin, President of Harris Stowe University, Dr. Juwan Warmack, Mr. Reynaldo Brown, Director of Admission, Florida Memorial University,

Dr. Michelle Thompson formerly of Bethune-Cookman University, Mr. Dennis Wright, and the 100 Black Men of Greater Fort Lauderdale, Ms. Jaquada Lee, Faith on Fire, The Texas Alliance of Black School Educators, The Preventing Crime in the Black Community Conference, Sponsored by The Attorney Generals Office of Florida, Ms. Beverly Morrison, Mr. Daniel Gillmore, Mrs. Vera

Warren Williams and The Essence Festival Book Expo, New Orleans, Louisiana, Thanks for Believing when no one else did. Mr. Anthony Jackson, Ms. Colleen Adams, Mr. Jerry, and Mr. Derrick of the Empowered Youth Program, and Career Services of South Florida.

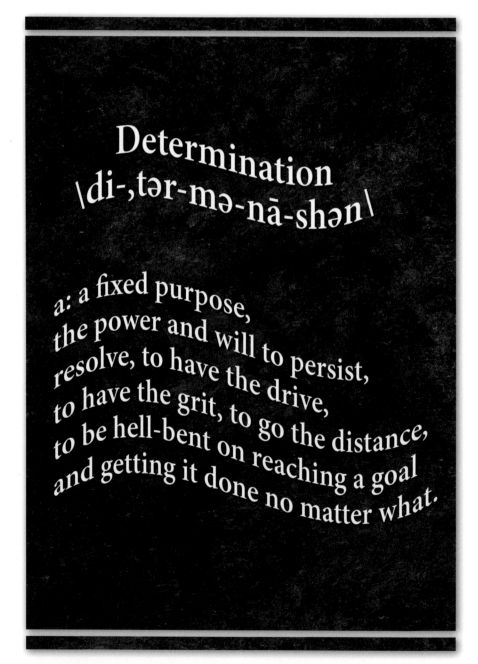

Determination
\di-,tər-mə-nā-shən\

a: a fixed purpose, the power and will to persist, resolve, to have the drive, to have the grit, to go the distance, to be hell-bent on reaching a goal and getting it done no matter what.

Inward Conversations,
Create Outward Realities!

The single most important conversation I ever had, was with myself. Most people are totally unaware of the fact, that our inner conversations are responsible for creating our outer reality. The **B**asic **I**nstructions **B**efore **L**eaving **E**arth states "As a Man thinketh, so is he," so a man's path of life, follows the tracks of his inner conversations. In order for one to take a different path, one must first change the old inner conversations with self, and be renewed in the spirit of the mind. By renewing the spirit of the mind, a new direction can be formulated. Life and Death are in the power of the tongue, therefore speech is the imagery and translation of the mind, awareness, or consciousness. In order to change one's mind, one must first change one's speech.

The speech is not the outward conversations that one has with someone else, but the inward speech or conversations that one has with ones self. This speech or conversation is responsible for creating the outward conversations with another. When we understand the importance and creative power of the inner conversations, we will regulate and monitor the conversations we have with ourselves as being vitally important. It is these inner conversations that are **constantly shaping** and **creating our reality**. Our outward reality is a direct correlation to the inner conversations that we are having with ourselves. As long as our inner conversations remain the same, our outward realities will not change.

Everything outside of man, must first exist inside of man. Our **internal** awareness and consciousness **attracts** and **creates our external realities**. Our inner and outer realities are one, and will always coincide.

There are no limits to our imagination, and our imaginations are able to create whatever we ask, in proportion to the degree of our belief, attention and ability. Especially with children and their development, nothing is more **important** than **imagination** to help enhance the growth of thought processes and creativity. All progress and achievement of desire is predicated upon ones ability to focus and control ones attention and efforts. Therefore, one must consciously choose to occupy ones concentration and attention on that which one desires. I am going to reiterate that statement again because it is extremely powerful, one must conscientiously and consistently choose to occupy ones concentration and attention on that which one desires. When we learn how to control our attention and thoughts, we now have more control of your world.

Read this 5 times in a row to make sure you truly understand it. Repetition is the mother of learning!

Understand, the conceiver will never
be greater than the concepts he conceives,
the believer will never accomplish, or receive
anything outside the realm of their beliefs, and we
will never rise above our highest level of thought.
Therefore, Life is What You Make it!

Read it again.

We have been given the ability to utilize our imagination and creative forces to create the world we desire. The Inventor can never be greater than the mental inventions stored in his consciousness or awareness. Who we are and become, is predicated on our mental state, our Mind Set, and how we utilize our mental state, or what our Mind is Set on, will create our reality and the life we live. Therefore the old adage, "Life is what we Make it" is actual and factual.

What are you creating?
As A Man Thinketh, So is He
—Proverbs 23:4

"Successful" sung by Trey Songz featuring Drake was a hit song I remember that spoke about Success. The hook of the clean version stated, "I want the money, money and the cars, cars and the clothes, I suppose, I just want to be, I just want to be Successful." When I first heard that hook, it really captured my attention, but it left me with one question. Why? Why do I want to be Successful, why do I want this stuff? Is acquiring stuff all there is to Success? Is there a deeper level of Success, than merely acquiring material possessions?

Don't get it twisted, I like nice things. However, I had been blessed with nice things before, and I was still looking for something deeper. It wasn't until I came to the realization that my Joy, Happiness, and fulfillment would be tied to my Purpose and the individuals I serve, that I began to look at my Success in a totally different perspective.

Blessings are Gifts and Talents that are given to us, but they are not necessarily for us. Our Gifts and Talents were given to us as Blessings, in order to be a Blessing to others. Truly Successful people are Successful because they aid in the Success of others. It is not what you have that makes you Successful, but how you utilize what you have to assist another in becoming Successful. If you are Successful, but have not helped anyone else become Successful, you are **Suc-Selfish**. Use the Gifts and Talents that you have been Blessed with, to be a Blessing to another. We are Blessed to be a Blessing. Never forget that.

Remember, the most important thing in your life, is HOW YOU SPEND YOUR TIME. So your TIME is the most important resource you have. I think you are at a point in your life where you are looking into your future and trying to figure out how you are going to get from where you are to where you want to be.

One thing I want you to understand is that getting there is a part of the process, and your willingness to embrace change, and take advantage of new and challenging opportunities will determine how much you grow, and how far you go. We must **grow** thru life, versus just **go** thru life. Many people want to change their external circumstances without changing inwardly. Our thoughts, actions, relationships and habits are things we must consider changing if we want our lives to change. We want to change our income, relationships, and even other people.

"We must grow thru life, versus just go thru life."

Again, the only way the outside world changes, is when our inside changes. Inside meaning our thought-life, our actions, feelings and habits. I have come to realize, once we become responsible for ourselves and our actions, we create our reality. In order to change as individuals, we must first change the information we receive, accept, and utilize. Then, we will have the ability to change our lives by CONSCIOUSLY understanding and utilizing the process of development to create our destiny or destination.

The information we utilize, plus the application of the information, creates our destination. I do believe you get out of life, what you put in to life. The question remains, how much do you want your life to change, and how much are you willing to change for your life? REAL TALK.

Mr. Hardge

Read, Believe, Do, Receive, Succeed.

You are a living
MAGNET
What you
attract into your
life is in harmony
with your
DOMINANT
thoughts.

—Brian Tracy

A BURNING DESIRE TO BE, AND TO DO is the starting point from which the **DREAMER** must depart into **ACTION**. Wishing and Praying alone, does not **CREATE** long term Health, Wealth, Prosperity, or Success. However, Health, Wealth, Prosperity, or Success, coupled with a state of mind that becomes an obsession, aligned with planning definite ways and means to create your desired result are the keys to Success. Aligning those plans with persistence, which does not recognize failure, will bring long lasting achievement, success, health, wealth, and prosperity. Yeah Man!

Morning Mantra

Today is the Best Day of my Life, because Today I am alive. I will maximize the moment, and utilize my time wisely. Being rich in Mind, Body, and Spirit is very important to me, and I will always align myself with this philosophy. I am grateful for Life, and the positive impact I have on the lives of others. I choose to be Healthy and Wealthy. I am Blessed, therefore, I will be a Blessing!

attract attraction

know now attraction

thoughts law

actions

world manifesting

power

always think

laws

every create

towards

words

reflection manifest miracle

desire

UNIVERSE today

future

manifestation

destiny

direct positive thought

master

want become

reality

Get Yo Mind Right!

*The kind of thoughts you are sending out,
determines what you are receiving in your life!*

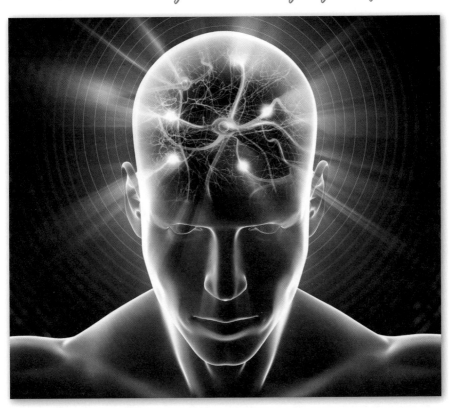

Our brain serves as an **antenna**, which transmits signals which are considered to be thought patterns, energy, or vibrations to the Universe. These signals attract things, situations, places, people, and information which corresponds, or correlates to the thoughts. patterns, energy, or vibrations, which **DOMINATE** our thinking and feelings. Therefore, our lives are directly proportional to the things we think about the most, and the feelings that **DOMINATE** our emotional state of being. The

1

only way to make changes of significant magnitudes in our lives, is to first make those changes that **DOMINATE** our thinking and emotions, which will create different decisions, actions, habits, and results. If we desire a specific result, we must make sure we align our **DOMINANT** thoughts and feelings with result we desire. Take a look at what you are receiving from the Universe, from life, more than likely, the same thoughts and feelings are **DOMINANT**.

We create our thoughts, feelings, actions, and habits, then our thoughts, feelings, actions, and habits create us!

Get Yo Mind Right!

Creation Principle 2

The 6 Types of People

I truly believe that we will never accomplish anything of great significance by ourselves. Therefore, we must collaborate with other individuals, and work collectively to accomplish or create major results. Even Jesus Christ, in all of his Majesty and Power, utilized the team approach by enlisting twelve disciples to go out into all the world and Preach the Gospel. Understand, two of his disciples betrayed him. Judas switched out for money, and Peter denied that he new him. These are perfect examples for us to understand, and live by. I have identified six types of people who you will encounter throughout this journey called **LIFE**, and your ability to discern the type of individuals they are, should dictate the type of relationship you should have with them.

Pilots

Pilots are individuals who have their own direction and agenda. These individuals are normally attractive leaders in some shape, form, or fashion. They are charismatic, and have a sense of self-worth or identity. However, they often use these gifts for selfish gain. They attract individuals who look up to them and turn them into Do-Boys as we called it back in the day. A Do-Boy was someone who did just about anything the Pilot said just to be down with them. The Pilot has only **ONE** mission, to get to a particular destination. Similar to you boarding a plane, the Pilot does not care who is on board and has always had a specific destination in mind. Nothing on board is going to deter the Pilot from arriving at the preplanned destination. Some people will enter your life, and **attempt** to take you where they are going. If the destination is not a destination you approve of, don't board that plane. Watch out for people who will try and control you and your life. If you don't control your life, some one else will. If you do not have a preplanned destination for your life, some one else will plan your life for you. As I recall, most of the problems I encountered as a youth, was due to me flying on someone else's plane, so it would behoove you to learn how to fly, and become your own Pilot. Every great leader is a great follower. If you are following someone, make sure you have the ability to get off the plane when you feel like leaving.

Passengers

Passengers are individuals who are only in your life, because they can't get to a particular destination on their own. We all need assistance to make things happen, and there is no "I" in TEAM. However, you should consider passengers as individuals who are just passing thru your life. When the going gets tough, they run. They are not there for you; they are there because you serve a Purpose pertaining to their own agenda. I am not saying we should not help people because we are blessed to be a blessing. However, passengers will ride in your car until you are out of gas, or your car breaks down, then they will find another way to get to their destination. If you had no means of transportation, they would not align themselves with you. They have their own agenda and destination in mind, and realize they need a vehicle to get there. That vehicle is YOU. They don't care about you; they care about how they can use you, to get to where they want to go. They will ride with you until you get them to where they want to go or until you can't, then, they will dismount, and find another ride.

Performers

Performers are really actors. They are individuals who will function as if they have your best interest in mind, as long as they are getting something out of the situation and are very similar to Passengers. However, these individuals are actually Passengers on steroids. They are similar to people who work for a company, an entertainer at a concert, or an actor in a movie. As long as they are receiving some type of payment or compensation, they will complete the performance and do it very well. As soon as they stop receiving something from you, they will find someone else to perform for. These individuals are similar to a leech. Performers are more difficult to notice then Passengers, because they are slick, smart, and crafty. Passengers will often leave you with a lil something, something because they just need a ride. However, Performers will suck you dry and leave you when you are on empty. They may actually like you, because of what you have to offer. It is customary to look for payment from your employer. However, it is detrimental if you have a friend, who is looking at you like you are an employer. As soon as the funds, good time, or whatever that you are providing stops, this individual is On to the Next One! Kanye West said it best "I Ain't saying she's a Gold Digger," but ahhh! Well you know the rest.

Predators

Predators are carnivores. They are individuals who will blatantly tell you in your face "I don't like you." You can't rationalize with a Predator, so don't try. Once you identify them as a Predator, accept it. They are individuals who are simply trying to stop you from getting to your destination, or your place of

Purpose. Also known as Haters, these individuals really hate themselves, and will stop at nothing to keep you on their level, because they are not moving forward, or going anywhere. As you **grow**, it **EXPOSES** other people's lack of **growth**, and makes them realize they are not growing. Thus your have the "Crab in The Bucket Syndrome." Watch out, there is a Judas in every arena. Predators can be deadly people, and their mission is to seek out and destroy anything or person they come in contact with.

Protégés

Good people create their own Success, Great people create the rest. Therefore, Success is actually about creating Success in others for others. Each One, Reach One, Teach One is a slogan mankind should embrace. Every person who truly understands the true definition of Success has a Protégé, and they understand the importance of grooming and preparing the younger generation for Success in any field of human endeavor. The reason we are Blessed is not to gloat, brag, or boast about the Blessing, but to be a Blessing. However, if you fail to have a Spiritual Connection with the Creator, you will worship the Creation, and look at the Blessing with a carnal mind and Ego. (**E**dging **G**od **O**ut). Understand, we are vessels that Blessing not only flow to, but thru. When you use your gifts, talents, skills, resources, and relationships to be a Blessing, you will always be Blessed. Successful people have Protégés. If you are successful and don't have a Protégé, then how Successful are you?

Partners

Partners are the type of individuals who you need to surround yourself with. These individuals are trustworthy and care about you as an individual, not about what you can provide for them. These are individuals who don't mind giving to you. Just make sure that you are a Partner as well, and not function in the Spirit of a Predator, Passenger, Performer, or Pilot. In a Partnership, there is a genuineness and synergy that exist. Commonalities serve as the foundation for the relationship, and differences do not create problems, but provide creativity, zeal, and fill voids and the inadequacies that exist within ourselves.

As I continue to grow and evolve as an individual,
there have been a few constants that stand out. Luke 6:38 says
"Give, and it shall be given unto you; good measure, pressed down and shaken together, and running over, shall men give into your bosom. For with the same measure that ye mete withal it shall be measured to you again."
Having the proper Partners as you pursue your Purpose, with Passion, is one of the keys to your Purpose and Prosperity.

Partners Feed each other, because Partners need each other. Yea man!

5

SOME PEOPLE PURSUE

Happiness,

OTHERS

Create It!

If Your

PRESENCE CAN'T ADD VALUE TO MY

Life

YOUR ABSENCE

Will Make No Difference

"If you can't fly, then run,
if you can't run, then walk,
if you can't walk, then crawl,
but whatever you do,
you have to keep moving forward."

—Dr. Martin Luther King Jr.

Creation Principle **3**

Mind
· · · · · · · · · · · · · ·
Matter

(Mind over Matter)

"Change your thoughts, Change your world."

—Christina Baldwin

ne of the greatest revelations that occurred in my life, is what I considered to be a moment of clarity. That's when I realized how my inner thoughts, attitudes, feelings, and actions, are responsible for shaping my world. I always thought our world, and all that exist

9

occurred by happenstance. When in all actuality, our reality is the direct result of three factors: our thoughts, feelings, and actions. What we think, will link to how we feel, and how we feel, will link to what we do, and what we think and feel strongly about, and do effectively, will create a **specific result**.

The picture you see on page 9 existed in the mind of the creator. It was a mere thought, which is necessary prior to the thought becoming a reality. Once the thought was linked to the **WILL**, and focused actions and persistence, the painting appeared. Everything that is **CREATED,** was first an idea in the mind of the **CREATOR**, before it became a **CREATION**. Therefore, everything in **CREATION** was **CREATED** for a **PURPOSE**. In the words of John "Crying Shame" Shaw, it's Mind Over Matter.

The secret workings of this life
are hidden from our sight.

It is the intangible things we can't see that creates the tangible, that which we can see. This is the starting point of **CREATION**. Everything starts inwardly first, then manifest outwardly. If success is what you truly desire, aligning your efforts with your **PURPOSE** is paramount. It is imperative you utilize visualization to assist you in accomplishing your goals and ambitions. Visualization is a mental technique that uses your imagination to create or develop images or dreams. These dreams must then be fed, nurtured, and acted upon to turn them into reality. Obviously, some dreams and desires are easier to manifest than others. However, your tenacity and ability to persevere will determine your outcome. Visualization can improve your life and attract success, abundance, and prosperity. It is a power that can alter your environment and circumstances, and can cause events to happen, attract money, possessions, work, people and love into our lives. The power of the mind is energy or vibrations, and is the power behind everything. Thoughts, when powerful enough, are planted and accepted by our subconscious mind, which causes a change in our present mindset, as well as our habits and actions, and this brings us into contact with new people, situations, and circumstances creating a new reality. Therefore, Life is truly What You Make it. Your life is made with your DOMINANT thoughts, feelings, and actions.

If you don't like what you are getting,
change your thoughts, feelings, and actions,
and this will change your results.

Nothing changes around us, until something changes within us. That's why INSANITY is defined as doing the same thing over and over and over again, then expecting a different result. Change is not easy, however, it is worth it, because you are worth it. You have to believe it, and be willing to **ACT** (**A**ction **C**hanges **T**hings). We must Fight until we can't Fight anymore. When you feel like you can't fight anymore, fight some more anyways. The individuals, who are able to motivate themselves beyond the limits of ordinary, are considered extra-ordinary. Hence the word extra, as a prefix to ordinary. It is one's ability to first know extra, and then do extra, to create the extra. Now that you know what it takes, what are you going to do?

Exercise

What is the major or primary aspect of your life you are going to change?

_____

_____

_____

_____

_____

_____

What do you need to know or learn in order to make the change?

_____

_____

_____

_____

_____

_____

What do you need to do (action) to make the change?

_____

_____

_____

_____

_____

_____

What are you willing to give up or sacrifice to make the change?

_____

_____

_____

_____

_____

_____

Who is going to assist or help you make the change?

_____

_____

_____

_____

_____

What group of people do you need to surround yourself with to make the change?

_____

_____

_____

_____

_____

How much of a financial investment is needed to assist you in manifesting your desires?

_____

_____

_____

_____

_____

" A people without the
knowledge of their past
history, origin and culture
is like a tree without roots. "

—Marcus Garvey

When the
Storms of Life come,
don't merely ask
for the Storms to
go away, ask for the

WISDOM

to undertand
how to Handle
The Storm, so the
Storm does not
Handle You.

Level of Expectations!

High achievement always takes place in the framework of High expectation.

—Charles F. Kettering

Expectation is a POWERFUL attractive force.
Expect the things you want, and
don't expect the things you don't want . . .

Giving thanks for what you want in advance
turbo-charges your desires and sends a more POWERFUL
signal out to the Universe.
—The Secret

Our beliefs and actions will create our expectations for the future. In order of importance, what type of expectations do you have for your future? Write them down on the next page.

What beliefs and actions do you have to change in order for them to align with your expectations? Write them down on the next page.

Our beliefs and actions will create our expectations for the future.
In order of importance, what type of expectations do you have for your
future? Write them down.

1. _____

_____

2. _____

_____

3. _____

_____

4. _____

_____

5. _____

_____

What beliefs and actions do you have to change in order for them to
align with your expectations? Write them down.

1. _____

_____

2. _____

_____

3. _____

_____

4. _____

_____

5. _____

_____

Law of Adaption!

*It is not the strongest of the species that survives,
or the most intelligent. It is the one that is
the most adaptable to CHANGE.*

—Charles Galton Darwin

Life is a Storyteller, and one of the stories I consistently see in my past, is a story about CHANGE. As I reflect on where I've been, where I am, to where I am going, CHANGE is a constant. Friends, family, material possessions, music, technology, everything is constantly changing around us. Therefore, it would behoove us to make some changes within ourselves, if not, we will end up glued to a certain time and space, because we did not evolve or change with the times. All of us know somebody who is glued to a particular time and space, because they failed to make the necessary changes that would have allowed them to make the transition into the present. It reminds me of when Martin Lawrence from the *Martin* show played a character named Romie Rome. This character was glued to the time and space of the 1970's, although he was living in the 1990's. He dressed, talked, and carried himself as if he was still living in that moment of time. Well, he was living in that time and space mentally, which caused him to express himself in that same manner. The failure to grow and evolve can cause a life of stagnation.

Change is inevitable, and can be for the better or worse. Our Society will change, our economy will change, even we as human beings will change. The key is being able to be ahead of the change, or in the midst of the change, versus behind the change. I am not speaking of trends that come and go, but the Mental, Spiritual. Emotional, Physical, and Financial development needed for us to continue to grow and evolve into our Super-Self. Being able to adapt to the changes around us that are beyond our control, is just as important as being able to make the necessary changes within ourselves that we can control. Some changes are forced upon us, and we have no say so in the matter. This is when adaptation is paramount. On the job, in school, in the community, or at home, some changes we are going to have to adapt to. Learn to live with Change, because Change is not going to Die. Change will outlive all of us!

• •

List 10 aspects about your character you should change in order to become a better person and why?

1. _____
2. _____
3. _____
4. _____
5. _____
6. _____
7. _____
8. _____
9. _____
10. _____

Change Exercise:

1. **Pontification:** What do you think you need to change about yourself or your life?

_____

_____

_____

_____

_____

2. **Contemplation:** Evaluate/analyze the change, and state why you need to make it.

_____

_____

_____

_____

_____

3. **Preparation/ACT:** Write out your plans to implement the CHANGE.

_____

_____

_____

_____

_____

4. **Maintenance:** Monitor your actions to insure they are taking you closer to the change you desire.

_____

_____

_____

_____

_____

5. **Accomplishment:** The change has become part of who you are, and there's no reason to return to the old ways.

_____

_____

_____

_____

_____

6. **Recycling:** You go back to **Contemplation** to determine if more change is needed. Understand, in order to remain CHANGED, you will have to continue doing the very thing that allowed the CHANGE to manifest. Read more:

_____

_____

_____

_____

_____

● ● ●

No one is going to come to your house and make your

DREAMS Come True.

● ● ●

It is not a Travesty to perish without accomplishing your **dreams,** but it is a Travesty to perish, without having any **dreams** to accomplish!

Every accomplishment starts with the decision to try.

accomplishment

" If we did all the things we are capable of doing, we would literally astonish ourselves. "

—Thomas Edison

"The function of education is to teach one to think intensely and to think critically. Intelligence plus character—that is the goal of true education. "

—Dr. Martin Luther King, Jr.

Creation Principle 6

Leadership!

*Leadership should not be measured by
one's ability to motivate, inspire, and lead ourselves,
but, by one's ability to motivate, lead, and
inspire others to become LEADERS.*

—Mr. Hardge

Philip of Macedonia, the father of Alexander the Great, said, "An army of deer led by a lion, is more to be feared than an army of lions led by a deer." That may be true, but I've come to believe that Philip missed the bigger point: An army of lions, led by a lion, is to be feared most of all, for it is unstoppable.

*G*ood people inspire themselves, Great people inspire others. Everyone who is a Great Leader, was once a Great Follower. We all are Leaders, the difference is who we are leading, and where we are going. I have come to the realization that **MONEY ALONE DOES NOT EQUATE TO LEADERSHIP**. Unfortunately, we live in a society that has been brainwashed with the belief, that if you are on Tel-**Lie**-Vision, or if you are rich financially, this qualifies you as a Leader. Most of our former leaders who truly impacted our world were not rich financially, or Tel-Lie-Vison personalities. Mahatma Gandhi, Nelson Mandela, Dr. Martin Luther King, Jr., Rosa Parks, Fredrick Douglas, Marcus Garvey, Malcolm X, Mother Teresa, Mary McCloud Bethune epitomized what I consider Leadership. They lead to bring forth change for others, versus to swell there pockets. I am all for entrepreneurship, for I am a BUSINESS- MAN. However, I will reiterate, making money does not make you a leader, unless your money is somehow impacting the lives of others, Philanthropy. Most Great leaders place the cause or purpose, before themselves. Leaders are visionaries, filled with the discipline and ambition to accomplish a goal, by soliciting the assistance of others, and for the benefit of others.

"Leaders must be close enough to relate to others, but far enough ahead to lead and motivate them."

—John C. Maxwell

The greatest leader of them all, was and still is, Jesus of Nazareth. His ability to motivate, relate, and create solutions for all who believed, and trusted in him is astonishing. He spent time with his leadership team, developing, teaching, and guiding them into becoming leaders. He was solutions-driven, led by example, and was filled with encouragement for all who would receive it. In spite of all of the challenges he faced, he never lost site of his Mission, and he constantly conveyed it, to ensure his purpose was not lost in the midst of chaos.

Be conscious of who and what you **CHOOSE** to follow. Make sure you are headed in a direction that leads to Health, Wealth, and the good things life has to offer. We must choose wisely, because there is someone following all of us.

> *Don't copy the behavior and customs of this world,*
> *but let God transform you into a new person,*
> *by changing the way you think.*
> *Then you will learn to know God's will for you,*
> *which is good, pleasing, and perfect.*
> —Romans 12:2, New Living Translation

Karma is Looking for You!

因缘 **Karma**

What you put out into the
world comes back to you.
How you live your life determines
what kind of life you will have.

J·A·Marie

irst and foremost, I do not subscribe to Buddhism. However, I do believe the Principle of Karma is relevant and applicable. Every time we think about something with great emotions, or do something consistently, we are creating a cause, which in time will bear its corresponding effects. We as individuals will be held accountable and responsible for our acts, feelings, and thoughts, whether we agree or not. The Universe shows no favor. Each person's karma is entirely his or her own, and we fail to realize that we receive the things in life that we give.

Every individual shapes their own future, by the thoughts, feelings, deeds, and actions of the present. Life is similar to a garden, and everyone plays the role of the gardener of their lives by the seeds they have planted. Sometimes, we inherit seeds from previous generations. These seeds are known as Generational seeds, and sometime we reap the harvest that we had nothing to do with the planting. However, in most cases, in due season, we will manifest a harvest of the seeds we planted. Your harvest will be totally dependent on the type of seed that you planted. Karma means action, and every action has consequences.

"Every individual shapes their own future."

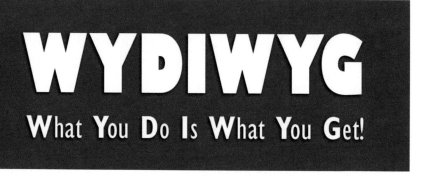

Do not be deceived, God is not mocked;
for whatever a man sows,
this he will also reap!
—Galatians 6:7

DON'T CREATE

BAD HABITS

"Education is the most powerful weapon which you can use to change the world."

—Nelson Mandela

Motivation thru Stimulation!

motivation
If there is a better reason to paddle,
I don't know what it is.

*P*erseverance, Energy, and Enthusiasm are the foundational traits that are tied to Motivation. What motivates one person, might not motivate another. However, you must find what will serve as motivation to you. Growing up as a youth in Ft. Lauderdale afforded me several opportunities to actually **RUN** for my life. My later teenage years were spent in the midst of the Crack Cocaine epidemic. The street life was very attractive to me, and I spent hours in the Hottest Spot in Town, the Inferno Lounge. This was where all of the Ballas partied. If you were somebody, or you wanted to be somebody, the Inferno was the spot. It was my first real taste of the night life, and it was exciting. Located in Hallandale, FL, it attracted people from Ft. Lauderdale and Miami. Money was everywhere, and all the Big Timers came out with Chunkies and old school Regals, Cutlasses, and Chevy's on Trues and Vogues. Chunkies were the Big Gold Rope chains like Run DMC use to wear. The Inferno was not a huge place, but it seemed big enough back then. With all that money and testosterone flowing in the building, something was bound to happen. What started out as a fight inside, ended up as a shoot out in the parking lot. As soon as we heard the shots, everybody hit the deck, or started running. I've played sports all of my life, but I never ran in sports, like I ran when I first heard those gun shots. I was truly motivated to run for safety.

"You must protect your Energy, Passion, and Enthusiasm."

If you are going to accomplish big objectives, you will need huge amounts of energy, perseverance, resources, and enthusiasm to create and maintain your motivation. The root word to motivation is motive. What is your motive or your why? What is the reason you are doing what you are doing? Your motive, or your reason or rationale for doing what you are doing must overshadow your failures or obstacles. You must protect your Energy, Passion, and Enthusiasm. Without these factors, it is almost impossible to remain motivated. Initially, money was my motivating factor. However, when I made my first million dollars in the Housing Boom from 2002-2008, I was not fulfilled. It isn't until I lost everything I had earned in Real Estate and Development, that Mr. Hardge found his Purpose, and that is to Educate, Motivate, and Enlighten our younger generation. To bring them into awareness that serve an awesome God, and All Things Are Possible, To Those Who Believe, and Love The Lord, Are Called To His Purpose!

I remember hearing a friend of mine Erik Rhett, former NFL Running Back tell his story at my first book signing. Mr. Rhett stated his main priority was to get to the NFL to get his mom off of the couch and buy her a new house. Other professional athletes who were born in Pro-Jects had the same goal, "to get their families out of the hood." Their success was to better the lives of their

32

family. It was not all about them, but about using their God-given talents to bless others. What drives you? What are you Passionate about? Who do you want to help? Whose battles are you willing to fight? You need to find out and focus on those answers pertaining to your Lifes-Work. Find your Purpose, it will keep you Motivated.

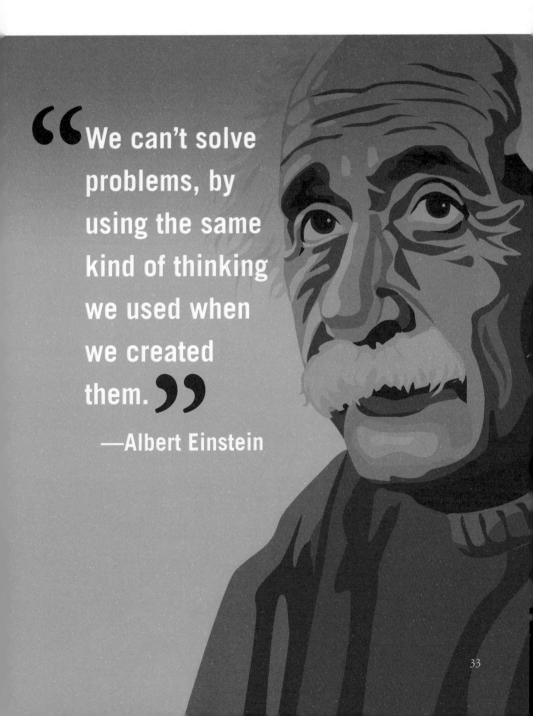

"We can't solve problems, by using the same kind of thinking we used when we created them."

—Albert Einstein

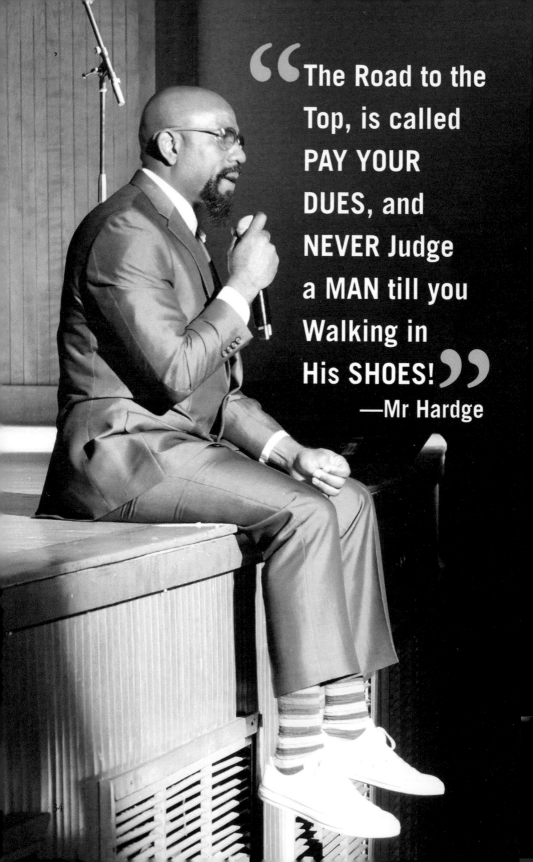

"The Road to the Top, is called PAY YOUR DUES, and NEVER Judge a MAN till you Walking in His SHOES!"
—Mr Hardge

Creation Principle **9**

Habitual Establishments!

Excellence is Habitual.
We are what we repeatedly do.
Therefore, Excellence, is not an act,
but a habit.

—Aristotle

The chains of habit, are too small to be felt . . . until they are too strong to be broken.

*O*ld destructive habits will never create new breakthroughs. We must unlearn invaluable information and actions, by increasing our knowledge base, and learning new content. This will allow us the opportunity to implement the necessary habits, disciplines, and actions that will produce the new outcomes we expect. Possessing a desire to produce excellent results is an innate or intrinsic quality. Excellence is not for someone else to notice, but for your own self satisfaction and gratification. Operating in excellence is an inward attitude that should permeate thru ones actions in every area of life. The desire to excel or operate in a spirit of excellence is not dependent on someone else being involved or being concerned. It's all about YOU. Mediocrity is doing just enough to get by, and if you do just enough to get by, that is all that you will get. Excellence is constantly exhibiting actions that are going to provide you with the results that are above average. Even if you don't get excellent results, that does not prevent you from striving for excellence.

"Excellence is the gradual result of
always striving to do better."

—Pat Riley

Life and school have an enormous amount of similarities. Both are filled with lessons, and in order to get to the next level, one must first understand the lesson being taught and then pass the test. The difference between living a life filled with excellence, or a life filled with mediocrity, is the individual who chooses to live a life of excellence looks in the mirror and recognizes their weaknesses as well as strengths. They operate in a spirit of truth, and constantly seek to better themselves versus trying to better their external circumstances. **They understand when they become better, there situation will become better.**

They understand when they become better, there situation will become better."

*We Create our Habits,
then our Habits Create Us!*

36

The desire to change themselves is the seed to a change in their situation. In spite of how bad the Chicago Bulls were as a team during Michael Jordan's first six or seven years, you could not deny Mr. Jordan's spirit of excellence on and off the court. He did not allow a bad team to make him a bad player. He was good enough to make a bad team look good. He operated in a spirit of excellence, with a work ethic that was beyond normal. He was extremely gifted, but he continuously worked on his gift. This actually explains why he was so great on the court. Champions are not made in the game with everyone watching, they are made in practice when nobody's watching. Success is not defined by never failing; it is defined by continuing to get up after you fail.

"Success is not defined by never failing; it is defined by continuing to get up after you fail."

Don't allow the failures of your past, to infiltrate your present, and pollute your future. You can break free of the entanglements of your past by staying focused on the opportunities and experiences of the present, and accomplish any goal you set for your future. There is a delicate balance to living happy, healthy, successful, and free. With dedication to personal development, you can manage this balance, and create a better you, by constantly and consistently walking in a Spirit Of Excellence. This means always striving to improve in all areas of your life. (Mentally, Spiritually, Emotionally, Financially, Physically). If you want to get the most out of life in every way, you have to put the most into it. This is a universal law that does not discriminate based on race, color, creed, gender, ethnicity, or religious belief. The Bible tells us that **you reap what you sow**. If you sow excellence in everything you do, then you will reap excellent rewards. The rewards may not be immediate.

However, don't allow the short-term discouragements to cause you to quit, because when you persist, you will prevail. It has to work this way. It is an immutable and indisputable law. If you know what successful people know, and do what successful people do, then you will achieve what successful people achieve. Remember, the key is to continually strive for excellence, continually striving to become a **better person**. Focus on the 3 P's, your Purpose, Passion, and Plan. In addition, always pray for Wisdom. Wisdom will allow you to make the right decisions at the right time, even if you make the wrong decision, now you know, and that's Wisdom. Wisdom also allows you to manage and become a good steward over the blessings you receive.

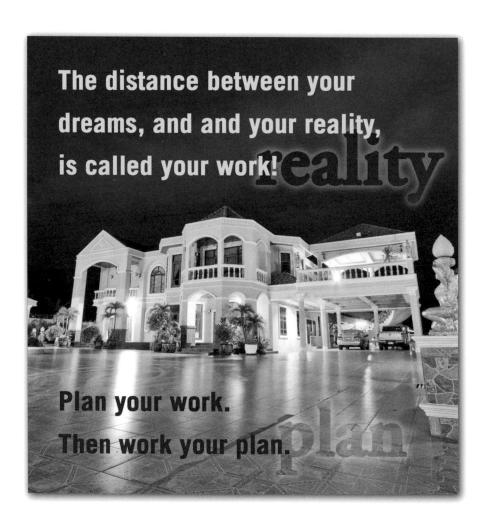

The distance between your dreams, and and your reality, is called your work! reality

Plan your work.
Then work your plan. plan

Positive Affirmation

I'm a Persistently Positive! I Grow! I Grow!
Despite being chopped at, poisoned, or pulled!
My Roots are Deep and are Alive!
I Thrive where others fail! I never give up!
I am a Persistently Positive Person!

I Rule the Garden of My Thought Life.

I attract

positive

people and

events into

my life

NOW

"A man who has no imagination has no wings. "

—Muhammad Ali

40

Creation Principle **10**

What You See,
is What You Will Be!

The person we believe ourselves to be,
will always act in a manner consistent
with our self-image.

—Brian Tracy

What **matters** most
is how you
see **yourself.**

A Positive Self-Image is the starting point of all Success. How we view the image of ourselves often determines the results we attract or receive in life. Our Self-Image is our own perception of ourselves. It encompasses the mental, spiritual, and emotional aspects of our being. Our thoughts about ourselves will create our internal attitude, and the way we perceive others. This inward perception will foster an outward view or filter of our world and everything that is encapsulated. If we have the wrong thoughts about ourselves, and if we are pessimistic, or negative, our external realities will correspond with our internal inadequacies. Our thoughts, feelings, emotions, environment, and associations are the building blocks for a positive self-image during the early childhood years.

As A Man Thinketh, So is HE!
—Proverbs 23:4

"I truly believe we are the sum total of all of our thoughts, feelings, actions, deeds, and experiences."

I truly believe we are the sum total of all of our **THOUGHTs, FEELINGS, ACTIONS, DEEDS, and EXPERIENCES.** As one thinks and feels, so they are; and as one continues to think and feel, so they shall remain. Therefore, in order to make constant or permanent change around us, we must first change the thought process, that serves as the seeds and action to our manifestation.

D-Termination!

"People of mediocre ability sometimes achieve outstanding success because they don't know when to quit. Most men succeed because they are determined to."

—George E. Allen

Anything is possible if you have the intelligence and willpower to make it happen!

*I*ntellect and financial resources are very important aspects pertaining to Success and Achievement. However, obstacles, challenges and setbacks are inevitable. At this moment, intellect, and financial resources can't replace being determined to overcome every obstacle that lies ahead. Determination is the quality of being motivated to do or achieve something. It is a common characteristic amongst high achievers. It is vitally important because it means that you are willing to do anything to overcome any and all challenges, just so you can achieve what you want; you are willing to see your project through to the end, despite any set-backs. Determination and perseverance move the world; thinking that others will do it for you is a sure way to fail. Continuous effort—is the key to unlocking our potential. People who soar, are those who refuse to sit back and wish things would change, they are determined to make the change by changing themselves and their actions.

"Determination and perseverance move the world; thinking that others will do it for you is a sure way to fail."

Success Ain't No Secret!

The only place Success comes before work,
is in the Dictionary.

Y ears ago, I was invited to speak at Silver Lakes Middle School by Mr. Vernon Dooling, to speak at a Young Men's Program for African American Boys. Mr. Dooling began talking to the young men about Success and hard work. He stated, "The only place Success comes before work, is in the Dictionary."

That statement fortified my understanding for hard work.

Success in any endeavor is not the end result of happenstance, wishing, hoping, or praying. To achieve true success, you need the strength of Mind, Body, and Spirit. Working hard and smart to reach your fullest potential is paramount. You need the right attitude, self-discipline, and the ability to put your goal before your own wants, if you are really driven towards reaching success. There is no substitute for hard and smart work, and according to Henry Ford, "The harder you work, the luckier you get"—the more successful you get! The results we receive, and what we achieve, will be in exact proportion to the effort we expend. Preparation is one of the keys to Success. Intense hard and smart work, along with great skills, shall help you win one success after another. There shall be innumerable obstacles on your path towards success. However, what makes a man truly worthy of the success that he attains, is the ability to remain FOCUSED, and continue FIGHTING, until he can reach his goal.

Work is an activity we all must partake in. Therefore, the key is to find the work we love to do. "Blessed is that man who hath found his work." If you are doing work you dislike, you will not reach your full potential, and all the treatments in creation can't make you succeed. If you don't love what you do, then go do what you love. Find your Purpose, this will cause you to live with Passion, and create a Plan for your Prosperity.

A Purpose filled man will keep trying and struggling until he perfects his art. Thomas Edison failed approximately 10,000 times while he was working on the light bulb, and yet he never dreamed of giving up. This is the hard work and determination that marks a true success. Indeed, success is not measured by the position that you are in today, but the amount of hard and smart work you put in, and the number of obstacles that you overcome to reach your goal.

"According to Newton's Third Law of Motion. Law number three says: For every action, there is an equal and opposite reaction."

More importantly, working smart is just as important as working hard. An intelligent working technique, along with relentless effort will go a long way in helping you achieve the success you desire.

A good work ethic is a commonality among high achievers and those who seem to get excellent results. Success can truly be measured by the person you become while on the road to achievement.

According to Newton's Third Law of Motion, Law number three says: For every action, there is an equal and opposite reaction.

What Newton was implying, was in order for something to happen, specific actions must take place. In other words if you want to create Success in your life, you must ACT. (Action Changes Things). On the other hand, if no action is exerted, nothing is created, or if the actions exerted are the wrong actions, you will get the wrong results. Doing does not necessarily mean you will get the desired result. Your actions must be proper to create the proper result.

Proverbs 13:4 says: "Lazy people want much but get little, but those who work hard, will prosper."

". . . if you want to create Success in your life, you must ACT. (Action Changes Things)."

It seems as if certain aspects of life have already been written for us. Most of our society will work 40–45 years before they have enough money to retire. In some cases, individuals are working well beyond their 60's, not because they want to, but because they have to. If you have to work, why not work at getting a larger piece of the pie. Who asked you if you wanted to wait until you are over 60 to retire? Did anyone ask your opinion pertaining to the way you want your life to go? Here is something to consider. If we are going to work, why not work at obtaining the whole pie, versus allowing someone to determine how much of the pie you deserve.

Life is what you make it.

Therefore, go out and make the pie you desire and deserve, otherwise, you will only get what others feel you deserve. You will always live in the world of a victim. Don't allow others to determine what you are worth.

Life is what you make it.

If you don't build your DREAM, someone will hire you to help build THEIRS.

You Are Exactly, Where You Thought You Would Be!

You are today where your dominant thoughts, feelings, and actions have brought you; you will be tomorrow where your dominant thoughts, feelings, and actions take you. Therefore, you are exactly where you thought you would be.

—James Allen

*T*he statement on page 49 is extremely powerful. I understand there are certain Economic, Political, and Spiritual influences that impact our destiny. However, the individual who became a Doctor did not become a Doctor by accident. The individual who became a Teacher did not become a Teacher by accident. Each had a definite purpose, and a followed a specific plan that created a specific result. Life is what we make it.

Therefore, the decisions we make or don't make, combined with the actions we take or don't take, make our lives.

". . . the decisions we make or don't make, combined with the actions we take or don't take, make our lives."

The Law of Attraction!

The Law of Attraction is a powerful perspective that I became conscience of. It states that things that are alike will be drawn towards each other, and things that are not alike, will repel away from each other. It matches things that are alike, not **unlike**, and similar to The Law of Gravity, is always at work. Imagine yourself as a GIANT MAGNET, and you attract what you think about the most, and feel the strongest about. We attract things, people, situations, and resources that are aligned with our thought process, vernacular, intense emotional feelings, which cause vibrations. Our thoughts also create words, feelings, and emotions, that are very powerful vibrations. These vibrations are constantly at work attracting things, people, situations, and resources that are responsible for creating our reality.

> *Life and death are in the*
> *power of the tongue.*
> —Proverbs 18:21

Positive thoughts and words create positive feelings, emotions, vibrations, and frequencies.

Positive Words:

Love, Joy, Compassion, Respect, Happiness

Negative thoughts and words create negative feelings, emotions, vibrations, and frequencies

Negative Words:

Hate, Jealousy, Poverty, Lack, Strife, Anger, Confusion

How do the thoughts and words you are using align with the Law of Attraction?

Based on the type of thoughts, words, emotions, and feelings we are emitting, we are attracting the same things, people, situations, and resources into our lives, which shapes our reality. If I am constantly thinking negative thoughts, and speaking negative words, these negative thoughts and words are creating negative emotions, feelings and vibrations. These negative vibrations are being sent out into the Universe as negative frequencies, and just like a giant magnet, these negative frequencies are attracting negative things, negative people, situations, and resources. It all began with the negative thoughts and feelings. However, the same will happen if when you have positive thoughts.

Our words as I stated previously, have power according to the Scriptures. Our words are energy, and function as frequencies and vibrations.

What you are constantly thinking and feeling, you are attracting!

What you are
constantly **thinking**
and **feeling,**

you are **attracting!**

    As I reflect on my childhood, teenage and early adulthood years, most of my friends were individuals who had the same interest or mindset. When I played football for the Western Tigers and Lauderdale Lakes Vikings, most of my free time was spent playing football with my friends who had the same mindset, and we were attracted to each other due to our commonalities. Playing football was very rewarding to me, in addition, I knew football players made an enormous amount of money, and I was determined as a youth to become wealthy.

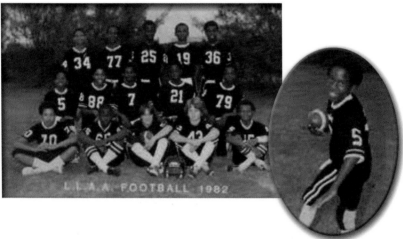

L.I.A.A. FOOTBALL 1982

As I entered Boyd Anderson High School, I was relatively small in stature, therefore, football was no longer an option. However, my desire to succeed did not, and has not diminished. During my 11th grade year, I played Junior Varsity basketball for the Boyd Anderson Cobras. I had a shift in my mindset, and started creating relationships with individuals who were interested in basketball. Football was no longer our priority; and due to the focus being basketball, a majority of my free time was spent with individuals who were attracted to the same sport. Now, do you think this is coincidental, or could a shift in my mindset, create a shift in my reality. The Law of Attraction states that things that are alike will be attracted to each other due to the commonalities. Plus, I knew basketball players made an enormous amount of money, I was determined to do the same.

Confidence Is A Stain You Can't Wipe Off!

During my senior year at Boyd Anderson, I was cut from the Varsity Basketball Team. I was devastated. I was always apart of some type of team structure, and didn't realize how much receiving positive reinforcement played in building my character. Eventually, I was asked to join a singing group called the Omni 5. We had desires to become successful entertainers, plus we knew most entertainers made a lot of money. Success and Achievement was, and still is a desire that resonates within my Spirit. We spent most of our time practicing dance steps and singing New Edition Songs. P-Nut, Dennis, Shawn, and Dallas, and I were the founding members, and we are still friends to this day. Why am I showing you these pictures and telling you this story? Well, on the road to Success, there are many opportunities to quit because things did not work out. However, I believe if you Fall

". . . on the road to Success, there are many opportunities . . ."

Down 9 times, get up 10. I have tried and failed many times, but I can, and will succeed as long as I keep trying. The goal doesn't always change, but the path to get there may. Don't stop fighting, you can win! The only person that can stop you from trying, is the man in the mirror. R.I.P. MJ.

Eventually, I thought back then that I ran out of options. I was involved in Football, Track, Bowling, Basketball, Singing and finally the streets. The Law of Attraction has always been at work in my life. As my mindset continued to shift, so did my affiliates and actions. When I started running the streets, my mindset, character, and goals totally shifted, due to a shift in my thinking. My thought process changed my feelings, and actions. My decisions changed who I chose, and who chose me as friends, and this began to shape a totally different reality. Hustle was the name of the game. My desire for Success and Achievement caused me to make some bad decisions. Actually, it was not just about the money back then, I was attracted to my team, my crew, my homies. Since I was no longer involved in sports, making money and avoiding 9 became the new game.

"The Law of Attraction has always been at work in my life."

I am not particularly proud of some of the decisions I made in the past. However, I am proud of the individual I became, in spite of some of my bad decisions.

"I am proud of the individual I became, in spite of some of my bad decisions."

Eventually, a few of my comrades were murdered, and a few of them ended up with 20, 30, or life sentences in prison. However, it wasn't until I almost lost my life and freedom, a light went off. A voice deep inside of my head while hiding in the trunk of an abandoned car, which is another story, said **"You are going to end up dead or in jail, do you care?"** Wow, I had been living recklessly, and making bad decisions, because I had given up on myself. I had accepted the creed of the streets. You will end up dead or in jail by the age 25.

How did I get so deep into a culture, that I was not necessarily born in? I was looking for a team, and wanted to be a part of something that made me feel good about myself, something that made me feel important. I wanted to be somebody, and wanted recognition for what I was good at. I truly believe, kids want, and need to feel good about themselves, and will get that attention, even if it is negative. We must build our children up with love, attention, positive, constructive criticism, while instilling values, morals, discipline, and the understanding of who God is. It was

"You are going to end up dead or in jail, do you care?"

God that allowed me an opportunity to make it out alive. He allowed me the opportunity to leave the snares of that trunk, and ordered my steps to Florida Memorial University. My entire life changed when I stepped on campus. I was a 21 year old freshman who needed a fresh start. I wanted my life to change, and I was willing to change for my life.

When I decided to make a change, and attend college, it was totally due to a shift in my thinking, feelings, and actions. The Law of Attraction was still at work, by attracting **things, people, situations, and resources that aligned with my current mental state**. Florida Memorial University served as a cocoon in my life cycle. A metamorphosis took place on that college campus, and if I wanted to continue to become the best I could become, I had to continue to change for the better. The Better-Fi-Cation process is ongoing. Now, it is clearer than ever before.

In 1995 I graduated with a Bachelor of Science Degree in Computer Science, and had evolved into a totally different person. The outward changes in my attitude, attire, actions, and character were a direct reflection of the inward changes in my Mental and Spiritual conditions. As I continued to grow through life, I continued to attract **things, people, situations, and resources** that were aligned with my current and future mindset.

"I continued to attract things, people, situations, and resources that were aligned with my current and future mindset."

The Paradigm Shift was gradual, but the shift was a shift nonetheless. Well, this is where my story really begins. 1996 was a new beginning for me, and I was ready for the world. My life had taken an amazing shift for the better, and I am thankful to God today for his Grace and Mercy that kept me. Well, the rest of my life has truly been an amazing adventure. I will pause here about my story because I want to get back to the real reason I wrote this book. I think you can see how the Law of Attraction has been at work in my life. After graduation, another Paradigm shift had taken place. I met some young brothers and sisters who were making between $30–$60,000 per month. They educated me on the importance of developing a mindset for success. They shared with me the importance of attending workshops, and seminars that educated you on how to accomplish your dreams and aspirations, how to select a business that provided you with opportunities to accomplish your financial objectives, and how Network Marketing can create financial independence. Shout out to Reggie and Erick Kennon, Herschell Gibbs, Troy Grant, and Randall "Skinny Benny" Jones. Teamwork really does make the Dream Work.

I did not make my first million in Network Marketing, but it prepared me to make my first million in real estate. Success Principles are applicable for life.

Success Principles are applicable for life.

Before

After

My company, Hardge Management Inc, acquired vacant land in the Washington Park and Roosevelt Gardens Sub-Divisions in Ft. Lauderdale, Florida, and built new single-family homes on them.

Although I made an enormous amount of money in Real Estate, I lost an enormous amount of money in the Real Estate Market when it crashed. At that point in time, my assignment was clarified and my Purpose was birthed. In spite of the downturn in the market, My first manuscript, Prescription For Success, 17 Principles for Success and Achievement was written, and I recorded my first album. In addition, I was afforded the opportunity to speak all over the United States, educating, enlightening, and inspiring individuals of all ages to design the life they desire. In addition, I believed, if I made a million once, I would do it again.

"In addition, I believed, if I made a million once, I would do it again."

Shout out to Miami Northwestern High School for a day of Edu-Tain-ment!

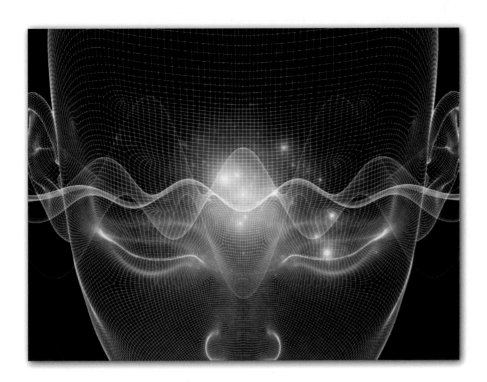

Remember, like thoughts attract like things. When you think and feel Healthy and Wealthy, things that are aligned with Health and Wealth often times come to you because the law works in a way that like thoughts attract like things. When you think and feel mistreated, fairness cannot find you because your perception of the mistreatment, and the vibration you send on a continual basis prevents anything which you would consider as fair to reach you. People may not be mistreating you, however, it could be your perception of people mistreating you. Now it becomes **your** problem. Change your mental antenna, emotional state, feeling, vibration, or energy, and you change your problem. When you think and feel poor or inferior, you begin to attract things, people, resources, and situations that are aligned with poverty or inferiority. The law works in a manner that like thoughts match like things.

"When you think and feel Healthy and Wealthy, things that are aligned with Health and Wealth often times come to you because the law works in a way that like thoughts attract like things."

This Law is consistent, it always gives you what you think about the most, and feel the strongest about!

Every man becomes, what he becomes because of the dominant thought he allows to resonate in his mind.

—James Allen

In order to experience change, you need to pivot your mind on higher or another frequency. (ex. change the position, from where your thinking starts) Wealthy people feel and think prosperity, success, and abundance, so they attract what they think about, and do. However, as soon as their thoughts change, the Universe will bring them those things in accordance to their thinking.

Poverty and Wealth are not merely a dollar amount, but a mindset. If Poverty was only a dollar amount, people who started out Poor, would never become Wealthy, and the Wealthy would never become Poor. Our thoughts and Actions create specific results.

"In order to experience change, you need to pivot your mind on higher or another frequency."

67

I accept and
ALLOW
SUCCESS
in all areas of
MY
LIFE.

Are you Conscious?

re you conscious of the fact that we either create our world or allow someone else to create it for us? Therefore, it is imperative we take 100% responsibility for our lives. It is important we choose an environment that will provide us with the opportunity to become the individuals we need to become to fulfill our purpose. We must constantly analyze our lives in terms of the information we are receiving, the individuals we affiliate with, and the environment we spend significant amounts of time in. Believe it or not, they are shaping us. Are the things and people around you helping you toward success, or are you allowing them to hold you back?

People who live with Purpose, or who are successful aren't born that way. They become successful by establishing the consciousness, and habit of doing things unsuccessful people don't do. The successful people don't always like the things they do, but they just do them anyways. It is okay to become Successful in an endeavor, and it not be affiliated with your Purpose in life. However, when you find your Purpose in Life, Success is inevitable, and you are fulfilled.

Every Thoroughbred is a Horse,
but Every Horse is not a Thoroughbred!

Creation Principle (16)

How I Got Away!

est, relaxation, restoration, and rejuvenation are much needed components for Success and Achievement. The MIND is a very powerful tool, and is the most powerful tool on Earth. It is **responsible** for every single **creation** we see.

Everything in Creation, was first Created in the MIND of the Creator, before it became a Creation. Therefore, everything was Created with a PURPOSE.

When the mind is being pushed to its limits, fatigue can diminish our creativity. Therefore, it needs time to refresh and replenish itself. Spending quiet time by the ocean is one of my favorite places for R-R-R-R, which is one of the benefits of living in South Florida. I am not totally sure of the location of the picture above, but it is truly relaxing. The only things we get in life are those things that we pursue. However, we must take time, to rejuvenate the Mind, Body, and Spirit, if we are going to function at our maximum potential. Work Hard, Play Hard, R-R-R-R.

"The only things we get in life are those things that we pursue."

Where there is a Will, there is a Way!

*O*perating with Ethics and Integrity are considered an integral aspect for Success and Achievement to me. How I get it, is more important to me, than what I get. The manner in which I ascertain my Goal is more important than the Goal I ascertain. However, the gentleman in the picture on page 73 is determined to create business for himself. I am not suggesting that we utilize underhanded methods to create what we desire, or do things that are unethical, but I am suggesting we utilize the same thought process, innovation, and creativity, to create our desires, with Integrity. Can you see how Dr. Unstoppable was able to create more business for himself, by creating a problem, that he served as the solution to the problem he created. I pray you get the message.

Mr. Hardge

• • • • • • • • • • • • • • • • • • • •

"Operating with Ethics and Integrity are considered an integral aspect for Success and Achievement."

Success and Achievement are based on several fundamental principles, one of those fundamental principles is having the ability to **Perceive** situations and circumstances properly. Being able to see problems as opportunities is vitally important. Analyze the collage of pictures on the previous page carefully. Trace Dr. Unstoppable's journey from pictures 1 thru 13. On a separate sheet of paper, identify and write at least 3 specific details pertaining to what is taking place in each picture, then answer questions below.

1. What type of problem does Dr. Unstoppable create? Explain.
2. How does Dr. Unstoppable solve the problem he created? Explain.
3. Do you think Dr. Unstoppable is conducting business with Ethics and Integrity? Explain.
4. When is it appropriate to sacrifice Ethics and Integrity for profit? Explain.

Creation Principle **18**

How Bad Do You Want It?

Overstand, nothing can take the place of persistence, not even Talent. Nothing is more common, than unsuccessful people with talent. Genius and Education alone, will not do it. The world is full of individuals, who have more Degrees than a thermometer; yet, they are not able to turn their education into something grander. Perseverance and determination alone are omnipotent. The Winners in life are not always the stronger or faster man, the one who wins in most cases, is the one who thinks he CAN!

Can't Stop, Won't Stop, Don't Stop!

persistence
Sometimes you've got to dig
a little deeper . . .

**MEDIOCRITY IS
UNACCEPTABLE.
LOW EXPECTATIONS
ARE A SIN!**

Creation Principle 19

T + A = R
Thoughts + Actions = Reality

*Our destiny changes with our thoughts:
we shall become what we wish to become, do what
we wish to do, when our thoughts corresponds
with our desires and actions.*

—Orison Swett Marden

The directions of our life will always be consistent with our thought processes and consistent actions.

As a Man Thinketh, so is HE!
—Proverbs 23:4

Get Yo Mind Right!

If **you** realized how **powerful** your thoughts are, you would never **think** a negative thought.

—Peace Pilgrim

WE NEED TO **TEACH** OUR

Daughters

TO DISTINGUISH
BETWEEN

A man who FLATTERS her
and a man who **COMPLIMENTS** her,

A man who SPENDS money on her
and a man who **INVESTS** in her,

A man who views her as PROPERTY
and a man who views her **PROPERLY**,

A man who LUSTS after her
and a man who **LOVES** her,

A man who believes he is a gift toWOMEN
and a man who believes she is a gift to **HIM**.

AND THEN WE NEED **TEACH** OUR

Sons

TO BE THAT
KIND OF MAN.

Co-Creators!

Man's rise or fall, success or failure,
happiness or unhappiness, depends on his attitude,
a man's attitude will create the
situation he imagines.

—James Allen

WEATHER YOU
THINK YOU CAN.
OR THINK YOU CAN'T.
YOU'RE RIGHT.
(HENRY FORD)

In the Basic Instruction Before Leaving Earth, it states we were made in the image or likeness of GOD, the Creator. As defined in the dictionary, the word image means: The state or fact of being **like** or **similar** to an original, and the word likeness means, possessing the same qualities or characteristics of an original but NOT replacing the original, because the ORIGINAL can't be replaced. Having similar attributes and qualities. Image, is the root word of Imagination. We are made in the Imagination of God, thru the imagination of God. If we were made in the image of God, the Creator, then we are to function in the same capacity of God, and Create thru our IMAGES, in our IMAGE-ination. Remember, Life is what you Make it! To make is to create. What are you creating?

WINNERS	LOOSERS
• Read Daily	• Watch TV Daily
• Set Goals	• Never Set Goals
• Compliment	• Criticize
• Embrace Change	• Fear Change
• Forgive	• Hold Grudges
• Talk About Ideas	• Talk About People
• Continuously Learn	• Think They Know it All
• Take Responsibility for Their Failures	• Blame Others for Their Failures
SUCCESS	**FAILURE**

Creation Principle **21**

The Gift!

The Past is History, the Future,
a mystery, the time we've been given
to live right now is truly a gift, that's why
it is called, the Present.

*D*uring one of my speaking engagements at the Preventing Crime in the Black Community Conference, sponsored by the Attorney Generals Office in Florida, a young man asked the question, "Mr. Hardge, what is the most important thing in life?" Suddenly, in no particular order, I began to think about God, my family, all of my material possessions. My business, my health, and a plethora of other

> *"Life is God's gift to us, and what we do with our life, is our gift to God."*

perspectives. After quickly contemplating all of the above, I realized, to me, the most important thing in life, is the Present.

Often times, we take our lives for granted, when the only time that we have is the here and now. The Present, today, is our only moment. Today will soon be yesterday, and tomorrow will be a new day. Therefore, we must realize the beauty in the NOW, and make the most of today because today is all we have. The time we spend alive, gives us the ability to partake in all of the amenities of life. Good Health is underrated, and should be at the top of everyone's list, and a sound state of mind is where it all begins. Living according to Biblical Truths, Universal Laws and Principles, Functioning in Wisdom, Love, Righteousness, and making the right decisions will determine the type of Life We Make for ourselves. Life is God's gift to us, and what we do with our life, is our gift to God. The greatest gift in life, is The Present. Today!

Don't take Your Present for Granted!

Neva Give Up!

"Most of the important things in the world,
have been accomplished by people who have kept on trying,
when there seemed to be no hope at all."

—Dale Carnegie

I once read "We Should Neva Give up on Something, if we can't Go a Day without Thinking about It." When you have a burning desire to achieve a goal, and you are having challenges achieving it, **NEVA GIVE UP**. Instead of giving up on accomplishing your goal, sometimes you have to change what you are doing, where you are doing it, and who you are doing it with. Making **MINOR** adjustments can create **MAJOR** changes in your results. Altering your actions will automatically create a different outcome. Obstacles are really opportunities in disguise. However, it is necessary to foster a **(PMA) P**ositive **M**ental **A**ttitude, to be able to view your obstacles as opportunities. Success and achievement have many twist and turns, and in most cases, you will have to make several adjustments to achieve, or acquire what you desire. I once read a quote that stated, "It is better to have tried and failed, than to never have tried at all." **It is in the TRYING, that you determine what works and what doesn't.** This is a part of the human experience, and this experience, or growth process creates a successful way of thinking and acting, and it develops good Character. It is the **Successful thoughts** and **actions** that create **Successful outcomes**. However, our goals will not be accomplished without action. In order for something to take place, you must **ACT**. (**A**ction **C**hanges **T**hings). When our consciousness or awareness expands, a paradigm shift takes place. This shift now provides us with the opportunity to view former obstacles as opportunities.

The Lack of Wisdom is the answer to most of our challenges. As we acquire more Wisdom, and evolve or grow mentally, we attract the end-results of our inward evolution and mental growth. Success is not determined by how many times you fall, but how many times you get up after falling. The greater the challenges you overcome, the more successful you will become. Think about it! In 2007, the real estate market plummeted, and Hardge Management Inc, which was my Real Estate and Development Company crashed along with it.

At that point, I was facing foreclosure on my home and several investment properties, and my new car and truck were being repossessed. One Sunday morning, as I was riding down I95 South in Miami, pontificating on how I was going to get out of this financial mess, a song entitled "We fall down, but we get up" by Donnie McClurkin started blasting over HOT 105. At that point, I decided to utilize my past experiences as a Success Story, and write *Prescription For Success*, and create a CD and DVD to motivate, educate, and inspire all who had a desire for Success and Achievement, even though I was loosing everything I had achieved. After completing the project, I started getting invitations to speak at Youth Seminars and Conferences all across the nation. One of the most important aspects of life is finding your **assignment** or **purpose** for living. I realized no matter how much money I made, or what I was doing in life, educating our youth would always be a part of my Life's Work.

That night, I began looking thru my old photo album, and began to reflect on all of the obstacles I had overcome as a youth. I believe there are three reasons I am alive today, the prayers of my mother, Grace, and Mercy. As I reflected on my past, I became overwhelmed with gratitude for God allowing me the opportunity to have achieve the type of Success I had achieved, in spite of all of my wrong doings. I was truly thankful for the man I had evolved into, and where I was in my life, in spite of my current financial conditions. The obstacles I was facing caused me to become more creative and innovative as well. My reason for becoming involved in Real Estate was to create financial independence. Even though the Real Estate market crashed, financial independence remained my goal, but my actions steps had to change if I was going to accomplish my goal. I had to create another plan, or find another vehicle, or opportunity that would allow me to create Financial Independence. The demise of the Real Estate Market taught me a valuable lesson. Your business investments and financial portfolio must be diversified. In addition, Bob Proctor from The Secret DVD made a statement that I will never forget. He stated, "if you want to become Financially Independent, you must have Multiple Streams of Income on a Continuous Basis." Most people have multiple bills that seem to visit every thirty days. Light bill, phone bill, water bill, mortgage, car note, insurance, daycare, and the list goes on.

However, we utilize one stream of income to pay multiple streams of bills. This simply is not logical. If for some unforeseen reason, we happen to lose our one stream of income, we no longer have money coming in to take care of our monthly expenditures. Now we begin to deplete our savings accounts and 401k's trying to survive until we ascertain another job. Been there, done that! We have to take more control of our financial future. However, this is no easy task, but it is possible. The true key to Success is finding and working within your Purpose. Therefore, it is imperative to work your job and your business, until your business income replaces your jobs income. This is not mandatory, but optional. This perspective is for those who desire or align with this perspective. It is not for everybody. We all have options. For that reason, I feel it is necessary to have Multiple Streams of Income on a Continuous Basis. Multi-Level Marketing, is another business industry that I chose to pursue. You can create significant amounts of money, but it is not only predicated upon your own efforts, it's a TEAM approach. When it comes to creating wealth, we have to utilize Wealth Principles. J. Paul Getty was a famous billionaire who said "He would rather have 1%, of 100 people's efforts, versus 100% of his own efforts when it comes to making money." One hundred people, will always outwork one person. Industriousness is vital for success because things are constantly changing.

". . . if you want to become Financially Independent, you must have multiple streams of income on a continuous basis."

Therefore, we have to constantly create and recreate ourselves, and our plans for the future. We must consistently evolve and develop mentally, physically, spiritually, emotionally, and financially. We have to prepare for the change, instead allowing the change, to change us. As you see, I face challenges and have obstacles just like you, but I will **NEVA GIVE UP**.

Mr. Hardge's 13 Traits of Highly Successful People

1 They don't expect more from others than they expect from themselves.

2 They understand the importance of utilizing their imagination and visualization to create a picture of the reality they desire.

3 They have a Purpose, Passion, and a Plan, and they make sure a majority of their time is spent on activities that are consistent with that Purpose, Passion, and Plan.

4 They utilize a Mastermind Group to accomplish their objectives.

5 They are open to new information, people and experiences. They are constantly evolving.

6 They understand a man will never rise above his highest level of thought, so Learning is on-going.

7 They have Uncommon Faith to an unseen reality.

8 They are Believers, Achievers and Receivers.

9 They are Doer's. They don't simply talk about it; they be about it!

10 They expend their energy and focus on actions that will produce high rewards.

11 They focus on the goals that are the most important.

12 They complete the task they started.

13 They maintain a Positive mental attitude and a positive vibration.

Success Test

A nswer the following questions. Go back and revisit each Principle for assistance or if you need help answering the questions.

Principle 1: *Get Yo Mind Right!*

The only way to make _____ of any magnitude in our

life is to first make those changes in our _____,

which will create different, _____

actions, and _____.

Principle 22: *6 Types of People!*

What are the 6 Types of People?

1. _____

_____

_____

_____.

2. _____

_____

_____

_____.

3. _____

_____

_____

_____.

4. _____

_____

_____.

5. _____

_____

_____.

6. _____

_____

_____.

Principle 3: *Mind Over Matter!*

What 3 things are responsible for shaping our world?

1. _____

_____

_____

_____,

2. _____

_____

_____

_____,

3. _____

_____

_____

_____.

Principle 4: *Level of Expectations!*

Why is it important to maintain the right level of expectations?

_____

_____

_____

_____

_____

_____

Principle 5: *Law of Adaption!*

What can cause a life of stagnation?

_____

_____

_____

_____

_____

_____

Principle 6: *Leadership!*

Leaders are _____, filled with

the _____ and _____

_____ to accomplish a goal, by _____

_____ the assistance of others.

Principle 7: *Karma is Looking for You!*

Every _____ shapes their own

_____, by the

_____, _____,

deeds, and actions of the _____.

Principle 8: *Motivation Thru Stimulation!*

If you are going to accomplish big _____,

you will need huge amounts of _____,

_____, and enthusiasm

to create and maintain your_____.

Principle 9: *Habitual Establishments!*

We _____ our Habits,

then our _____ create us.

Principle 10: *What You See, is What You Will Be!*

What is a Self-Image? Why is a Positive one important?

_____

_____

_____

_____

_____

_____

_____

Principle 11: *D-Termination!*

The key to unlocking our potential is?

_____

_____

_____

_____

_____

_____

Principle 12: *Success Ain't No Secret!*

The only place Success comes before work is where? _____

_____

_____

_____

_____

_____

Principle 13: *You Are Exactly, Where You Thought You Would Be!*

You are _____ where your

_____ have brought you;

you _____ will be

_____ where your

_____

_____ take you.

Principle 14: *The Law of Attraction!*

What are vibrations constantly doing in our lives?

_____

_____

_____

_____

_____

_____

_____

_____

Principle 15: *Are You Conscious?*

We must constantly _____ our lives

in terms of the information we are _____,

the individuals we _____ with, and the

_____

_____

we spend significant amounts of time in.

Principle 16: *How I Got Away!*

The _____ is the most powerful tool on.

_____

Why? _____

_____

_____

_____

_____

_____

Principle 17: *Where there is a Will, there is a Way!*

Would you consider this gentleman to be an innovator? Why?

_____

_____

_____

_____

_____

_____

_____

_____

Principle 18: *How Bad Do You Want It?*

The _____ in life are not always the stronger or faster man, the _____ _____ one who wins, in most cases, is the one who thinks he _____!

Principle 19: *T+A=R Thoughts + Actions = Reality!*

Explain how our Thoughts + Actions = Reality.

_____

_____

_____

_____

_____

_____

_____

_____

Principle 20: *Co-Creators!*

Do you think the quote for Henry Ford is true or false? Explain your answer:

_____

_____

_____

_____

_____

_____

_____

_____

Principle 21: *The Gift!*

What is the Gift?

_____

_____

_____

_____

_____

_____

_____

_____

_____

Principle 22: *TNeva Give Up!*

In order for things to change, we must ACT. ACT is an acronym.

The A means _____, the

C means _____, and the

T means _____.

Attitude of Gratitude

What Things are you grateful for and why:

1. _____
_____
_____
_____
_____.

2. _____
_____
_____
_____
_____.

3. _____
_____
_____
_____
_____.

4. _____
_____
_____
_____.

5. _____

_____

_____

_____

_____.

6. _____

_____

_____

_____

_____.

7. _____

_____

_____

_____

_____.

8. _____

_____

_____

_____

_____.

9. _____

_____

_____

_____

_____.

10._____

_____

_____

_____

_____.

11._____

_____

_____

_____

_____.

12._____

_____

_____

_____

_____.

13._____

_____

_____

_____

_____.

14._____

_____

_____

_____

_____.

15. _____

_____

_____

_____

_____ .

16. _____

_____

_____

_____

_____ .

17. _____

_____

_____

_____

_____ .

18. _____

_____

_____

_____

_____ .

19. _____

_____

_____

_____

_____ .

20._____

_____

_____

_____

_____.

If we desire to attract more into our lives, it is important we become appreciative of what we have already. Having an Attitude of Gratitude is a wonderful quality to operate in.

> *"If you are faithful in little things,*
> *you will be faithful in large ones. But if you are*
> *dishonest in little things, you won't be honest*
> *with greater responsibilities.*
> —Luke 16:10, New Living Translation

The future belongs to those who see possibilities, before they become obvious.

—John Scully

vision

What you can achieve is limited only by how far you can see.

motivation

Overstand, for every result, or desired outcome, there is an adequate, and definite cause or action. Therefore, when a given result is desired, one must seek the cause or action, by which this result may be created, or attained.

The Master Key System

On Earning

"**Never depend on single income. Make investment to create a second source.**"

On Spending

"**If you buy things you do not need, soon you will have to sell things you need.**"

On Savings

"**Do not save what is left after spending, but spend what is left after saving.**"

On Taking Risk

" Never test the depth of river with both feet. "

On Investment

" Do not put eggs all in one basket. "

On Expectations

" Honesty is very expensive gift. Do not expect it from cheap people. "

#Life Is What You Make It!

#DreamsDoComeTrue!

#GoAndGetIt!

I Would Like to Thank My
FLORIDA MEMORIAL
Family

FLORIDA MEMORIAL COLLEGE

Presented
To

Darrel Hardge

OUTSTANDING DEFENSIVE
AWARD

1993 - 1994

 FLORIDA MEMORIAL COLLEGE
1994-95

Presented To

Darrell Hardge

Outstanding Offense Award

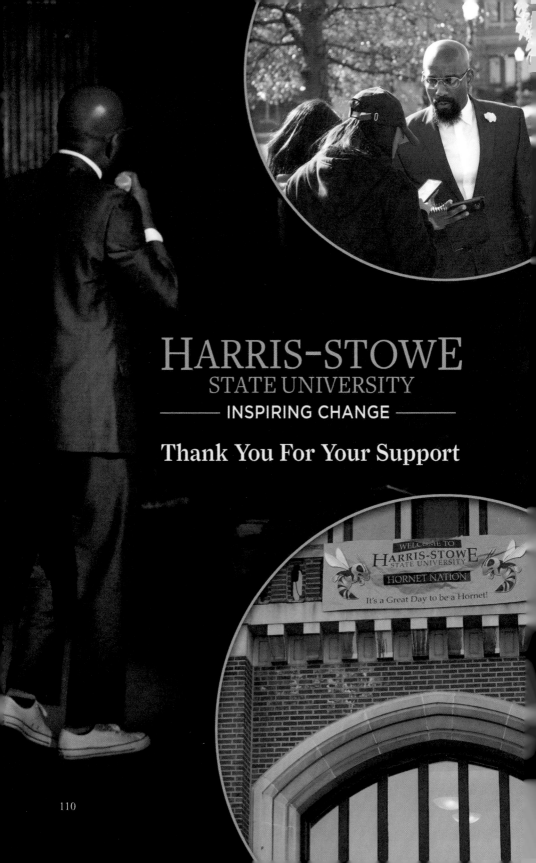

HARRIS-STOWE
STATE UNIVERSITY
— INSPIRING CHANGE —

Thank You For Your Support

Real Men Giving Real Time®

| Home | About Us | Press Center | Sponsorship | Membership | Photos | Contact Us |

WHAT THEY SEE IS WHAT THEY'LL BE®

The 100 The 100 Black Men of Greater Fort Lauderdale welcomes you to be a part of an organization that is making a serious commitment to elevate the Black Family by addressing our Four For The Future.

Members of the 100 Black Men of Greater Fort Lauderdale all share the common goal of improving the economic status of our communities as well as providing programs that enhance and enrich lives through Mentoring, Education, Economic Development, and Health and Wellness. Members of this orgnization will positively influence lives by serving as positive role models.

News and Events

Leadership Academy

Located at:
Nova Southeastern University
3301 College Ave.
Davie, FL 33314
Saturdays from
10:00am -
12:00pm.
It's not too late to register.

FOUR FOR THE FUTURE

Mentoring
Education
Health and Wellness
Economic Development

100BMOGFL PROGRAMS

Leadership Academy
What's Your Swagger
Million Father March
100 Annual Bike Drive
100 Scholarship
Online Tutoring

www.100blackmengfl.org

Inspire, Empower, and Transform!

Vision

Our vision at Whiddon-Rogers Education Center is to become a nationally recognized school of excellence in innovative educational alternatives designed to prepare students for college and careers.

Mission

Whiddon-Roger Education Center's Mission is to provide appropriate alternative educational strategies and resources that support social emotional growth and instill a desire to become lifelong learners.

Whiddon-Rogers Education Center
700 SW 26 Street • Fort Lauderdale, FL 33315
754.321.7550 • 754.321.7580 fax
whiddonrogers.browardschools.com

To order books, or
Speaking Engagements and Workshops

MrHardge@MrHardge.com

954-444-8000

www.MrHardge.com